RISE

and

SHINE

Whimsical, Evocative Inspirations
about Love, Life, and Transformations

A. J. Chandler

BALBOA.
PRESS
A DIVISION OF HAY HOUSE

Balboa Press books may be ordered through booksellers or by contacting:

Balboa Press
A Division of Hay House
1663 Liberty Drive
Bloomington, IN 47403
www.balboapress.com
1 (877) 407-4847

Print information available on the last page.

ISBN: 978-1-9822-2795-1 (sc)
ISBN: 978-1-9822-2796-8 (e)

Library of Congress Control Number: 2019906854

Balboa Press rev. date: 07/27/2019

Contents

Acknowledgement

I would like to thank and acknowledge the two gifted artists who not only blessed this book with their beautiful artistic illustrations and photography, but who also provided me with much encouragement and inspiration for this book. I love you!

Jackson L. Ball, Nature Photographer from AffinityStudio.net
Taylor Green, Freelance Artist from TGGalleries.com

Introduction

Writing poetry is nourishment for my soul.
I used to write poetry for fun when I was in my teens and twenties, but never again, until now, more than thirty years later. So what happened?

As you may suspect, it took me experiencing that "dark night of the soul", a place where we are often called to take a good look at our lives and ourselves, and begin to ask the hard questions:

Are we living the life we desire? Do we have the kinds of relationships we yearn for? Do we have a life that is balanced in work, play and social connections? Are we healthy and vital? And, why do we have fears and doubts and how do we overcome them? Just what is keeping us from being the best version of who we are and living our best life ever?

Through my own personal journey, I not only found profound answers to these questions, but also rediscovered poetry as a way to communicate them. This way of expressing myself provided much growth and healing from the inside out. Also, as an empathic person, I feel the vibe of the planet intensely which is why I express worldly feelings in many of these poems.

Sometimes we are called to step outside of our comfort zone and do a little soul searching in order to discover the best part of who we are and why we are here.

I share these "poetic emotions" in hopes that you too will be inspired to RISE and SHINE, as we all are called to stand up and raise our frequency and amplify our light across this beautiful planet.

With Peace, love & Joy!
Angie

"Poetry is when an emotion has found its thought and, the thought has found words."

~ Robert Frost

Soul Rocker

Soul rocker come rock my soul I prayed so many moons ago
The great-spirit listened, and sent one who shook me high and low.

From the depths of my soul
to the heights of my spirit, he led the way.
I followed, got lost, then stayed close so we would never stray.

This is a soul-rocking, karmic, love-hate, pain, ecstasy kind of thing
Revealing a powerful love and leaving a familiar sting.

I drop to my knees and ask the great spirit
to teach me what this means
Then listen with my heart as I release those
limiting beliefs and old scenes.

This happy ending is not like the others,
with the two hearts finding their lost twin.
This is a story about a soul rocker who finds
love when the two hearts both win.

They win but lose. They hurt but feel alive.
They feel deeply and always will.
This soul rocker kind of love is for a purpose much greater than the hill.

The dream is alive as they climb the hill from where they say goodbye
They release the weight and spread their wings and both begin to fly.

This story ends and begins with the two becoming one
When they rock their souls alive and victory is won.

"A great relationship doesn't happen because of the love in the beginning but how well you continue to build love until the end."

~ anonymous

Same Love
Different Way

Give me the same love
in every way every day.
Not a different love one way
and another today.

Give me a love that is deep
and grows like a wild vine.
Ascending up a beautiful tree
getting stronger with time.

Show me love one way every day
And, surprise me along the way.
Keep me longing for that same love
in a different way.

Give me love that lasts
a lifetime and more.
That same love we
remember from before.

Give me your love and only your love
forever and a day.
An equal love that gives
and receives in every way.

Give me your love
in your way every day.
That same love I love
in a different way.

"Communication to a relationship is like oxygen to life, without it…it dies."

~ Tony Gaskins

Let Me Know You Inside Out

Let me know you inside out
What makes you tingle and want to shout?

What makes you laugh and want to play?
And, kiss the skies and dance the night away?

What makes your soul feel safe and alive?
Ready to thrive, not just survive.

What brings you joy and sets your heart on fire?
Let me know, so we can savor and take it higher.

What makes you feel safe and secure from pains of the past?
Or trust someone to hold you and give you a love that lasts?

Let me share all of me with all of you, and you with me
The good, the bad and the all that is part of we.

Nature Photography by Jackson L. Ball

Wrong Time for Divine Love

Is this a sacred union given at the wrong time
Or a true love that will always be divine?

Standing at this crossroads and blocking our path
Where do we go?
We run, we chase, we open then close
We feel up then down like a yo-yo.

Did this sacred union lose its heart?
Or was it destiny playing a role
with a crazy part?

No doubt, this love is sincere and very real
It is here to serve and to heal.

Let's take our lessons learned, and embody them like Christ
We will try again, when this love can melt all of the ice.

It's now time for us to ascend to a higher place
Loving ourselves like we love the other in each and every case.

This may seem like a wrong time for divine love
But it is never a wrong time for sacred love to rise above.

Nature Photography by Jackson L. Ball

Sunrise Surprise

I sit in silence in the wee hours of the morn
Staring at the stars and the moon feeling torn.

This great universe and I conversing from above
Speaking to me from deep inside on what I need to love.

How, what, when and where will I ever know for sure?
This hanging on and never knowing if this love is pure.

The back and forth and uncertainty of it all
Leaves me feeling lost and confused by this fall.

As the the moon fades and the stars begin to stray
I realize just how God works and provides in a mysterious way.

When the morning light rises and shines across my face
It shows me why I'm here, at this time, and in this place.

The confusion from the past is gone and never coming back
I simply lean forward, breathe, and live without any lack.

Feeling free to be me, a perfect human soul learning to heal
What a surprise when dawn becomes day
and the sun ignites this love I feel.

"Self-love is the source for all other loves."

~ Pierre Corneille

Love From Within

From the beginning I knew
I had found a true love and life mate.
The one who would bring real love
brought by divine fate.

I was a woman who was strong
And knew her value and self-worth
But got lost inside this love for us
and died to experience a rebirth.

This resurrection day was a beginning
of living in a brand new way.
The blindness to the illusions
becoming clearer by the day.

I was no longer a lost and wounded child
seeking to feel love.
I am now an enlightened soul
finding answers from within and above.

The love for myself renews
And rejuvenates from deep within.
Opening a portal to self-worth
And an understanding on where to begin.

I no longer sacrifice the depths of my soul to only love you
I now find love from within as you may too.

Love found deep inside the heart
is a like a precious tea.
It is when we drink from this cup of self-love
Our souls are set free.

"It takes courage to grow up and to turn out to be who you really are"

~ E.E. Cummings

Transformation Day

I will always remember my transformation day
A day the earth stood still and the illusions fell away.

A day of truth and illumination to living in an enlightened new way
A way to live in peace, love and joy every day.

We all can shift, change and live lives in our own way
A life that lifts the spirits and awakens our hearts as we laugh and play.

It's time we transform into something better than our current way
And choose to live in unity and co-create together every day.

A day of transformation is a celebration shining bright like a sun ray,
Living creatively, igniting passion and with a love that is here to stay.

We are here to be ourselves and not let others get in the way
The day we say yes to living life our way
is the ultimate transformation day.

"We shall nobly save or meanly lose,
the last best hope for earth"

~ Abraham Lincoln

Evolution Revolution

It does appear that we are here
to evolve into something great.
To be part of a revolution for evolution
that we all get to create.

Inside our mother's womb
we rest, and begin our journey to evolve
Then, at birth
we release our souls to soar
to shine and never to dissolve.

We humans like to call it evolution
and accept the good with the bad.
When in fact, this evolution
is really transformation, unlike any we've ever had.

Unlike the babies we used to be
with eyes of innocence that saw only the best
We simply evolved into fearful beings
from the sickness of our society's test.

Let them scare us and test us
But never control the human pool
For we are emerging into something stronger
And no longer play the fool.

We are evolving back into the human souls
we came here to be
We are waking up and remembering
who we are as we all become free.

To have freedom to be all that we are
is worthy of any revolution
One that is based on love, higher consciousness
and is a divine resolution.

"When the power of love overcomes the love of power, the world will know peace."

~ Jimi Hendrix

We as a Human Race

We as a human race are seeking refuge from
bombs and fighting for no reason;
We as a human race are waking up to all the manipulation and treason.

We as a human race pledge to protect our land, our people and our souls;
We no longer surrender to what we are told
or the divisions caused by polls.

We as a human race choose to get out of our
heads and think more with our heart;
We are waking up and will never again accept
those things that kept us apart.

We as a human race choose a better way to make our countries great;
We as a human race believe in the power of love,
Not the destruction of hate.

We as a human race are returning to love and trusting in a higher power;
We release and detach from those in the dark tower.

We as a human race forgive those who have
deceived us in the name of freedom;
We now free ourselves as we expand in our divine kingdom.

We as a human race accept the changes we must make
And live to give and receive, not just take.

To be human is to feel and be real in body, mind and soul;
We were never to be a race divided and separate,
only one unified and whole.

"A little anti-war poem written with love"

A Battlefield of Love

Are we choosing a battlefield of love or fighting in lands of hate?
When will we choose freedom of peace and
not remain victim to deceptive bait?

Why is it that we continue to experience unnecessary fears and greed?
Can we not see that the love for our planet, ourselves and each other
is all we need?

Let us not pretend that the power of love is not enough,
for love is not always soft and sweet,
it is sometimes tough.

Our world today is calling for us to stand up
And be proud of the power of love
To live in victory every day
from the strength we find within and above.

Our battlefields are no longer the ones where we send people to die
Nor are they the ones based on years of betrayal from a big fat lie.

We're waking up, and choosing battlefields
that do not kill or harm mankind
Instead, we choose battlefields of love
and fight with a strong heart and healthy mind.

No more wars that destroy and detach us from our super-powers above.
We will win the war, when peace is made on the battlefield of love.

A World Insane

By Artist Taylor Green

A World Insane

To live with inner pain is just insane
Yet people live with it everyday in vain.

So many people choosing death over living
Losing hope, because there is a lack of giving.

My heart aches to see our country in all this pain and weeping
People living with daily stress and worries, keeping them from sleeping.

We're so very blessed to live on this planet
that exudes such beauty and grace
Still, we have allowed it to be morphed into a messed up heartless place.

Everyday we are bombarded with news of shock and horror
Lost souls sacrificing life, because they see no better tomorrow.

It is now time to stop fighting and competing for status and wealth
We need a place where our emotions and feelings create our good health.

Drugs, alcohol and toxic foods killing us all, the young and the old
We must remember, God gave us everything
we need just as we were told.

No more wars and illnesses erupting from a people in pain
Let us rise above and never again live in a world insane.

Nature Photography by Jackson L. Ball

Under the Clouds

Under the clouds we can escape this place of chaos and stress
And allow the elegance and softness to heal with each caress.

It's a remarkable thing to see and feel nature's beauty and soul
A place to look up, converge and merge with something whole.

Under the clouds the sky appears so very close, yet so far away
Shapes and pictures calling us closer, enticing us to stay.

We can easily sense these majestic forces coming from the divine
And drawing us closer to peace, love and joy perfectly in time.

The experience of oneness with our universe is truly a marvelous feat
It is mystical, magical and produces a feeling that is hard to beat.

So if ever you have a day of monkey mind with thoughts that scatter
Just go sit under the clouds and take in some of this universal matter.

Beneath its beauty and grace, our thoughts gently and freely drift away
Leaving behind an inner peace that lasts throughout the day.

"Sometimes you never know the meaning of a moment until it becomes a memory."

~ Dr. Seuss

It's Now or Never

Beauty is often found in some of the most profound ways
The blossom inside has yet revealed its true colors or its new day.

We live here today as if we are here forever
When will learn that it's now or never?

Life does not wait for those who are lazy
Life says come on, let's get a little crazy.

Sometimes, we just need to throw a little caution to the wind
Step outside our comfort zone and make a new friend.

There's no time for regressing back to old ways of living
We are here to chill out more and really start living.

No more stressing and living in lack
Let's bring some of that good ole fun back.

Remember, we only going around once in a lifetime
Why not dance, sing, laugh and play, for it's not a crime.

Be yourself no matter what, be it shy or be it clever
Just remember, you are here for you, and it's now or never.

"Music is so much more than something that entertains,
It rejuvenates the mind, body and soul on a deep vibrational level."

Rock n Roll Revival

Oh how that rock n roll music makes us feel and groove
Touching us deep inside, freeing us with every move.

The rhythms and rips filling us up with pure total bliss
Enticing us to dance and sing and hug and kiss.

When the soul knows it's time to laugh and play
It will go out of its way to be in those frequencies any day.

When life presents those ups and downs that help us grow
This is the perfect time for a little rock n roll
to bring back some of that old glow.

If the heart's been broken in a million pieces and can't seem to feel
This is a great time to immerse in some musical waves to help it heal.

Music is so much more than something that entertains the soul
Music is a sacred and magical tool that opens us up and makes us whole.

So next time you're feeling out of sorts, or that life is taking its toll
Just go to your happy place, and revive your soul
with some good ole rock n roll.

Nature Photography by Jackson L. Ball

High Road to Heaven

When we take the high road to heaven
It doesn't matter if we're seventy-five or eleven.

We all know what is wrong and what is right
We can see and feel the difference between darkness and light.

It's true, we no longer need to try to be
All we are is all part of We.

We have our light and we have our dark
And sometimes the bite is not as bad as the bark.

There's really no need to live in fear from what others might say
We're here to live in our truth, with love and integrity, each and every day.

The golden rule is all we ever really need
It is simple, and easy, and Jesus planted the seed.

Let's take the high road to heaven and ride it all the way to the end
Staying on course, living in truth, around each and every bend.

"Things do not change, we change."

~Henry David Thoreau

Coming Alive
at Fifty-Five

It is said, that the number five represents transformation and change
All I know, is fifty-five knocked me completely out of range.

This magical number revealing itself to me as some kind of joke
Taking me to a place with a nurturing hold and an unexpected choke.

I felt the pain and confusion of bursting out of an illusion
My heart opening, and my spirit rising to allow this fusion.

The emerging of something different and very new
Like waters of purification, washing over me in a sea of blue.

I sense a love for myself and for others like never before
It is time to open up and come out of the closed door.

The time is here and the season is ripe
With gratitude for the journey and for the tears to wipe.

Feeling fresh, alive and excited to begin this new ascent
My heart opens wide and ready to receive all that is heavenly sent.

So whether you are fifty-five or younger or older
It is never too late to come alive, and live a little bolder.

Nature Photography by Jackson L. Ball

Blind Journey

They say that life is a journey and not a destination
One that can seem blind and often lead to frustration.

A journey back to self is confusing and not easily seen
We learn to surrender and keep the faith to discover the dream.

God drops us breadcrumbs in little winks and nudges along the way
Leading us down uncertain paths, even when we may want to stay.

A blind journey may seem like a crazy way to live a life
Never knowing for sure what lies beyond the walls or the strife.

The silence inside can often sound loud, yet, be peaceful and sweet
While nurturing the pain avoided, until finally its time to meet.

Self-discovery can take us places where we sometimes have to merge
Allowing our soul to let go, and let God, and maybe even purge.

The journey back to self is never a smooth ride
Often times, we are forced to take the waves and just follow the tide.

Yes, there will be obstacles and setbacks along a path or two
Best to come along on this ride with no expectations except finding you.

Look Who I AM
By Artist Taylor Green

Look Who I AM

Why do we live in a world where it's look what
I have, instead of look who I am?
Or look at my title and my position, rather than,
look at my creation and intuition.

One day, I believe we will figure it all out
And have the freedom to be all that we are
Liberated as we release and shout.

It's not our doing and pushing that makes things happen in our favor,
It's when we take the time to feel, to be inspired,
and taste the foods we want to savor.

Who I am is all there is, and if you know who I am you too will be found
For who we are is all that we are, and shall be.
We are the mountains, the sea, the air and the ground.

We are the yin and the yang
We are the here and now, and we are always on time.
We are both the spirit of the masculine and feminine divine.

So put down your technologies and begin to rest your mind
For when we are in harmony with ourselves
we are more loving and kind.

We treat others the way we want to be treated,
because that is the golden rule
No more judging or fighting, or behaving like a fool.

Let's look beyond what we can see or think
And simply feel, listening to those inner nudges and winks.

Ask me who I am, and I will tell you with love
All that I am is everything that I am, here below and above.

"He who knows that enough is enough
will always have enough."

~ LAO TZU

Mama Blues

Ever had a crazy mama who made you feel the blues?
For what its worth, you're not alone, for we all have been there too.

We are the kids who all grew up without a mama around
She's in the house making sounds, but where's
the encouraging support found?

Our mamas are pretty and loved by many and that is a very nice thing
She dresses us up and takes us out to play and dance and sing.

It seems the grades are good, but never good enough
Always wanting to achieve more or be better can make life tough.

Over the years we learn to shield and protect the heart from feeling blue
We never tell just how we feel, because we thought she really knew.

We grow up good and acting bad to become what we think she wants us to be
We do everything for everyone to receive the love we crave you see.

The crazy mama is not so bad, nor is she really just crazy at all
She is really one of us, all grown up, teaching us not to fail or fall.

She has lots of fears that create the tears and that is the crazy part you see
If only she knew just how much she is loved and accepted by you and me.

So in the end, we finally begin, to learn to pick and choose
We simply love ourselves even more, from our crazy mama blues.

Nature Photography by Jackson L. Ball

This Deep River

A twin flame union is a very "Deep River," at least that's what was told
As soon as we embraced, we felt a special kind of hold.

Who knew we would fall so deeply or under such a spell?
A feeling to remember, never trade it or ever tell.

The journey began from the very start while standing on a dock
Under the stars, in the saltwater air, our hearts began to lock.

I was blown away and feeling shy
You too, we knew, by the look in the eye.

Our hearts began to merge and the flames ignited
We felt the familiarity as our souls reunited.

We had never known or experienced such spiritual ecstasy before
Two hearts, two souls, merging wide open as they begin to soar.

Indeed, the twin flame journey is a very deep river
A once in a lifetime love, that makes us tingle and quiver.

It is where waters run deep, with rocks and rapids along the way
Always flowing to the peaceful part, where we can stay and play.

Heart of a Woman
By Artist Taylor Green

Heart of a Woman

It is the heart of a woman where graceful powers lie
At times, it lies dormant and other times free to fly.

It's a special power, where sweetness is strength and softness is profound
Where sensitivity creates more, and attracts the highest energies around.

The heart of a woman is where the voice of God is often heard
Sometimes, only as a whisper, and can even sound absurd.

The heart of a woman is our ability to listen with the heart
It is here the answers to the questions and the creation for the art.

The heart of a woman is not just for the girls
It is also for those loving men who share in these pearls.

When we love from our hearts and listen with our innate
We quickly see just how love and its power can overcome hate.

We know how it feels to be nurtured like a baby
We also know what it s like to be abandoned maybe.

What I know is what I feel and all is well and shall be
An amazing power of love found in the heart of a woman like me.

Winds of Change
By Artist Taylor Green

Winds of Change

It is during the winds of change that we grow the most
A gust of wind appearing from nowhere, like a ghost.

The winds come howling and sounding like an angry God
Pouring its wisdom over us, even sounding a bit odd.

The winds of change can sometimes bring an unexpected twist or turn
Taking us down uncertain paths, where we must learn to trust and discern.

We choose to believe and listen to what these winds have to say
Because we know that God is powerful and can speak to us in that way.

When winds of change come blowing in and swirling all around
It means to simply surrender, and let the answers be magically found.

We simply trust that we're divinely protected and that's enough
No need to have fear in times that are rough or with negative stuff.

We open and welcome change, for it delivers exactly what we need
Not always what we expect, many times it is far better indeed.

So the next time you experience a magical breeze sounding a bit strange
Just remember, it may be the perfect time, for some winds of change.

"Can I get an Amen?"

Free Souls Are We

A collective of souls are we
A part of God that is one and free.

We live in union with everyone, whether or not we believe the same
We choose free will and transform with love and not shame.

Our existence is really more than what we think we know
There are other worlds on the other side, and we can go.

We are here to live as one, and be part of something grand
A time in history more powerful than any other on any land.

.

Our human race is now changing, and evolving into something more
A metamorphosis of mankind, unlike anything we've ever seen before.

Like butterflies, we too are transforming into new life
One that is vibrant and healthy and free from strife.

We must live to thrive and not just survive
For this is how our living God stays alive.

We are a trinity complete in mind, body and soul
We can no longer let life keep us down or take its toll.

Our souls are free, and waking up at this time and in this place
To usher in a new era, one for human consciousness and inner space.

Changing ourselves from within creates a
good for all, and that we must do
To be both the student and the teacher, as we restore, revive and renew.

We are human, we are vibration, we are frequency, and we are light
We are souls who are free to resonate, amplify,
and reflect a light that is bright.

"When we send love in response to hate
We become spiritual alchemists."

~ *Wayne Dyer*

When Wrong is Right

When did we drift so far away from what we know to be right?
When did wrong become right and the darkness over shadow our light?

We are all children of God and have a right to be wrong
We also have the right to be who we are, and sing our own unique song.

We are here together, whether we like it or not
So, why don't we just join hands and give one love a shot?

No more hating or judging the other for what we don't know
Let us take care of our own lives and stay in our own personal flow.

So whether you prefer black or white or red or blue
We are really pure light, living as one love, in consciousness too.

All the great masters taught us well, to have compassion, and not to hate
They showed us how to love, to relate, and to communicate.

We just got lost along the way in this crazy game of life
But now, we thrive, not just survive, as we let go of fear and strife.

In the end, we all want the same, and that is to live a life that is right
To live in peace, love and joy, even if we have to fight.

"Alone we do little, together we can do so much."

~ Helen Keller

Returning to Love

Returning to love is what is being asked of both you and me
We are to expand in consciousness and follow a path that is free.

We must now become the one we have been waiting for
And embody our great master's Spirit as we begin to soar.

When we return to love in both word and deed
This is when we find all we truly need.

No more fears of being alone or not having enough
We are here together, and can make it through any and all stuff.

We all know that God is love and love is God
So why do we question love as if it is something odd?

We are born as pure love, and that is how we must choose to be
We are to be happy, healthy and whole, in peace, love and harmony.

Let's heed what God's Spirit would have us to do
For that is how we show him a love that is true.

We create heaven on earth when we return to love
It is then, we live happily ever after, down here, and above.

Nature Photography by Jackson L Ball

Mountain of Faith

Along this journey we call life, some roads are easy and others are tough
Some have rocks and thorns, others bring flowers and beautiful stuff.

We say we believe and follow a holy creed
So, why do we doubt in those times of need?

Some people get scared, run and seek ways to hide
If only they would remember to let go, flow, and ride the tide.

Believing in something unseen always boggles the human mind
Until, we discover the magic in the miracles left behind.

We were told to ask in order to receive
Maybe it's time to practice those things we believe.

Along this journey, we learn to trust in what may seem obscure
Using only faith as our inner compass, known and secure.

It is said having faith of a mustard seed can move a mountain
What a great a time to drink from this over flowing fountain.

Next time uncertainty arrives, creating fears and shadows of doubt
Just surrender to this mountain of faith to find your way out.

"The happy man is the one who has a healthy body,
a wealthy soul and a well educated nature"

~Thales

Money Matters Not

The good book says we cannot worship two gods
So, why do people try to live against these odds?

Egos with unconscious capitalism never saved a nation
Nor, has it ever led to a positive creation.

May we find a happy middle ground and build something new
A place that is fair and equal to everyone, not just a few.

I will work hard to do my part, and hope that you will do the same
We need much more in this life, than just quick financial gain.

We need to bring love and respect back to each other
Live creative lives, and be more accepting of our brother.

When we find happiness from within and not in the external things
Life becomes truly abundant and we are free to fly with wings.

It is sad when one loses their dignity and soul
Just to feel special or loved when life takes its toll.

We don't need diamonds or pearls
We need people who makes us shine and twirl.

We are here to be rich in love, not to hoard and collect our lot
The truly wealthy understand, that money matters not.

Nature Photography by Jackson L. Ball

Magic in the Molting

There is great magic in the molting of our feathers
It is where we slow, shed, and prepare for different weathers.

The weight of the old worn out wings sometimes must go
There comes a time when we must release the tow and just flow.

A time to shed any fears of past, present and future that hold growth back
And let the layers be peeled
One moment at a time, until there is no more lack.

We learn as we grow, to let be, to evolve and let things change
Our job is to surrender and embody the lessons,
no matter how hard or strange.

We practice self-love and accept the skin we
are in as it ages, sags and flaws
And, gracefully embrace these new feathers
that now match our wise claws.

"*Aging is not for sissies*", I heard an old friend once say
The secret is to maintain balance, work hard,
then let go and play along the way.

The years will come and go as we shed,
transform and fly with our new wings
Just remember, there is magic in the molting, for it brings in fresh new things.

Nature Photography by Jackson L. Ball

Mother's Cry for Earth

She awakes and looks around, when her eyes fill with tears
The disrespect and destruction from years of greed and fears.

Deforestation, animal poaching and over building for wealth
Never a consideration for our wellbeing or the future of our health.

Our great mother has come to speak in the only language we understand
She ask that we pay attention, or pay the price
of losing more than our land.

This land is holy, and given to us all, not just a few
It is meant for everyone to enjoy, and love, and protect too.

A mother's job is to give birth to a life where it can thrive
Not to put money in pockets of those who destroy to survive.

Our great mother earth provides so much for our needs
If only we would work with her, rather than stripping her to weeds.

The sun, water and wind have the power to generate for years to come
All we need to do, is support these natural gifts,
And allow the creation of some.

Mother earth's love is unlike any we have ever known since birth
It is why we can feel her pain, when our mother cries for earth.

Nature Photography by Jackson L. Ball

Generations

Generations go by one by one
Leaving their mark on the daughter and the son.

Each child with its own journey in life
Yet, still bonded regardless of a husband or a wife.

Years go by and the lessons begin
We learn that we are here to love, not just to win.

The father passes his knowledge and his skills
The mother with her wisdom and caring frills.

The years become teachers as we evolve and grow
Making us stronger as we find our own flow.

Each generation leaves a trail for the next
With hope that this new one will be the best.

So pay close attention to these generations please
Because, each one leaves a permanent ring in the family trees.

"Sometimes we just have to let go and let God"

Surrender

If we can't be the real thing then why be it at all?
For that would be settling for less and risking a huge fall.

The best kind of love is the kind where we feel good and should
Not be yearning and hoping for the love we thought we could.

It is time to be strong and lean forward as we make our way to the other side
Where we meet with a love that is bigger and stronger and can heal any divide.

This kind of love does require a trust and a faith much greater than before
It is a crazy bond that never breaks, even when it hits the floor.

I once asked the great mother to teach me how to have this kind of trust,
She simply said, just remember who you are, and surrender, it's a must.

Surrender to love with love and leave the rest to you know who
This is how we find the love that makes me, me, and you, you.

Nature Photography by Jackson L. Ball

Free to Fly

We are free to fly because love is here to stay
We get to drop the stressful days and have fun and live to play.

To soar, to shine and transform into the very best version of I
No matter how hard the tests, or how high we must fly.

This story is mine, yours and ours for as long as we choose
It is time for us all to write a different script, one without the blues.

Our country, our people, our family and our friends are all here
waiting for us to extend our wings and fly without fear.

We are here to find our way back and remember what the great masters taught
To love thyself, be true to you and remember we are not the wars we have fought.

All of us are here in one way or another to learn to fly
And, expand in consciousness and embody a frequency that is high.

We are grateful for the lessons learned along the way
for that is how we find the courage and freedom to stay.

Never under estimate the power of inner knowing and listening with the heart
This is how we honor our soul's purpose and build a love that will never part.

To spread our wings and fly like a bird is the greatest feeling of all
It is what expands and propels us to be free to fly without a fall.

*"Our desire to choose greatness requires
our willingness to choose to love"*

Love is a Choice

We are entering a crossroads and the choice is ours
We all are being called to do the hard work.

It is a shedding of the things that no longer serve us
And a letting go to allow for the beginning of new growth.

It is not for the weary and weak, it is for those
who are strong on the inside
And, who can reflect it on the outside by how well they walk the talk.

How strongly we express love, show love, is
more important now than ever before
Our gift of free will is being challenged at a significant pace
Our desire to choose greatness requires our willingness to choose love.

Choose love over being right
Choose love over irritation
Choose love over impatience
Choose love over judgment
Choose love over anger
Choose love, if love is what you desire.

Love can only live when it is fed and nurtured with love
Love loves to love. Love is all there is and ever will be.

Who we choose to love is a reflection of ourselves
Because, we choose to love the part of us that needs love the most.

As we reflect back the need for love
Often, through anger, fear and control
We learn to love those parts of ourselves too.

The scared little child who needs love
The pain that needs love
A heart that needs love

Love is the most powerful healer.
Love is a choice.

Nature photography by Jackson L. Ball

From Flux to Flow

Ever wondered how some people just move through life with ease
Rarely becoming stressed or angry or living with disease?

I have learned over the years by watching and observing the best
And what I saw, are those who simply take on
life challenges as some kind of test.

Some are young and some are old, regardless of age, they are bold
These are the people who live life by their terms
And not by what they are told.

When life brings them ups and downs, they
simply take a breath, and turn it around.
They understand how to stop and pivot and not get stuck or bound.

Moving from a state of flux with a gentle nudge from deep within
Allowing us to find a more peaceful place to come out with a win.

To flow in life requires a positive state of mind
Treating you in a way that is kind, learning to relax and unwind.

So next time you feel that life is in chaos and you have no place to go
Simply remember, the best way to move through it, is to go from flux to flow.

"Quality is not an accident.
It is always the result of intelligent effort."

~ John Ruskin

Remember When

Remember when we were kids and it was safe to play?
How nice that would be if we could have this for our children today.

A world where we could trust our neighbor, our sister and brother
One where we would remove all walls that
keep us from loving each other.

The time has come to drop the technologies and run for the hills
It is time to climb up mountains and run down
beaches to find our joy and thrills.

Remember when we could talk to one another and look in the eyes?
Share a real connection, or be there when a friend or child cries.

Remember when the food we ate really tasted great?
Not like the crap today full of the artificial stuff we hate.

Let's go retro in ways we remember, and bring
back the qualities that made us real
To live a life where we are happier, healthier
and no one would ever need to steal.

Remember when we could buy a product that would last for years?
Not the cheap stuff we have today, that makes us mad and shed our tears.

We need to bring back the things that were made with high integrity then
And, replace what we do today with the things that make us remember when.

"Honesty and transparency make you vulnerable. Be honest and transparent anyway."

~ Mother Theresa

Keeping It Real

Let's be real for a moment or two
And, discuss those things that are needed for me and for you.

Sometimes it is ok to pretend and play
But, when it comes to being real, we must mean what we say.

It is always best to say what you feel
Never apologize for keeping it real.

When we genuinely live an authentic life
That is when we are free from pain and strife.

If we are always trying to be, rather than, just being the be
We will never understand the things that make us free.

It is when we approach life in a way that matters without the frills
It is then we are happy, because we choose to live life keeping it real.

Rise and Shine
By Artist Taylor Green

Rise and Shine

Let us rise up to become the best version of us
Shining our light as we fly above all of the darkness and fuss.

There comes a time when we are called to pause
Lifting ourselves up, and fight for a positive cause.

Never again allowing the burdens of the world to make us weak
Instead, we rise up, stand tall and climb to the top of the peak.

Together we are stronger, and no longer accept greed and fears
We find strength and power in making peace as we wipe our tears.

As a people of God, we should never ever feel weary and weak
For we are much greater than that, and can find the strength we seek.

It is time to rise up in spirit and live the life we came here for
Shining a light that is bright and illuminates from our core.

Like a sunrise emerging, and tasting better than fine wine
We get to start over, and become more as we rise and shine.

"Only passions, great passions can elevate the soul to great things."

~ Denis Diderot

Elevate

The time has come for us to rise up and elevate
And join our light and really resonate!

The world is watching and cheering us on
It is up to us to vote for what's real
And not a con.

Let us focus on who we are and why we are here
We are now blessed by a new era
And should never ever fear.

Those who know the force of God and the power this light
Are now getting ready to usher in something that is very bright.

Like the stars we are, it is time for us to shine
And elevate our lives to a level of a fine bottle of wine.

We can dance and sing and express our joy
We can play like kids with their favorite toy.

Lets' look forward to what tomorrow can bring
And keep our faith on the thing that makes our heart sing.

As we elevate in mind, body and spirit, we ascend to a brand new place
A destined and higher dimension, one that soon we will face.

We no longer have to try to be, we just are, it is fate
That is why we must choose to be free and just elevate.

Final Thoughts...

"Whether it's the power of the mind, the power of belief, the power of vibrations, the power of intention or the power of love; What has now become clear to modern science, and is becoming clear to more of us by the day, is that there is great power within us; And, the time to exercise that power, and to do so together, has come."

About the Author

A.J. Chandler is a former healthcare and pharmaceutical professional of twenty years and was a spa owner for another decade. She is a student of business, spirituality and science, and is currently researching emerging concepts for inner fitness and wellbeing, which led to her own personal journey of self- discovery.

She is also the founder of Joi Center, where she is collaborating with others to build a place for inner fitness and optimal wellness, both as an online platform and as a destination place.

This book evolved during a one-year period of letting go and expressing her feelings about personal growth and the world at large. She enjoys traveling to many countries living the life she writes about and shining light on how we all can live life more fit from the inside out, both as individuals and as a collective.

You can learn more at **riseandshine.website**

Printed in the United States
By Bookmasters